CRACKED POTS

Allowing God to Turn your Flaws into Blessings

Holly W. Smith

ISBN-10: 0615884768
ISBN-13: 978-0615884769

Awakening Truth Publishing

For privacy reasons, some names in Cracked Pots have been changed.

Back cover photo by VJ Photography

Cover design by Chris Schell

PRAISE FOR CRACKED POTS

Just wanted you to know how much I enjoyed the session [at Hope Center in Plano, Texas] with Holly Smith entitled *Cracked Pots*. I don't have a sister but I could still relate because everyone has compared themselves with someone, at one time or another. I thought it was fascinating the way the Lord revealed to her EXACTLY how to overcome the inferiority and competing with her sister for attention. I could tell that Holly conquered this issue within herself. I believe this is a great message for women in this hour. The enemy is using EVERY TACTIC possible to keep women trapped below the surface with any feelings that he can use. If the enemy can keep us down with these envious feelings or offenses, then we can never be used by God the way He intends. I feel Holly should write a book called *Cracked Pots*. God confirmed this when she actually discovered pottery that was cracked and then transformed into a beautiful piece of pottery. I really enjoyed her testimony!

-Carelynne Johnson

"This is not a teaching about facts but the Holy Spirit changing us. Holly knows what she is talking about because she has plowed the ground, preparing the way for others."

-Colleen Foshee–*Booming Women*

"Allowing the Holy Spirit to guide her, Holly's teaching *Cracked Pots* conveys God's desire for His children to find freedom. This is a balanced and sound biblical teaching about how we find freedom by allowing God to work within our painful experiences from the past. Holly's humbled heart and complete transparency awakened in me a thirst for God's truth in a new way. This teaching is a must for anyone with a desire for a *true* spiritual awakening."

-Ronda Parker

DEDICATION

Dedicated to God, who patiently caused me to gain understanding and knew what was best for me.

2 Corinthians 12:9 *My grace is sufficient for you, for my power is made perfect in weakness. Therefore I will boast all the more gladly about my weaknesses, so that Christ's power may rest on me.*

In honor of my dear brother and best friend, Mark, whom I hoped to help but will meet again; to Laura and Bonnie, who died much too soon and are greatly missed.

To Nana and Mama, who taught me love, courage, and dignity.

ACKNOWLEDGEMENTS

Thanks to my mom and sister, whom I admire and love dearly and have been so generous with me. Appreciate the final proofing work. You are amazing.

Thanks, love, and hugs to my dad who has always been there for me.

Appreciation and love to my husband, Alan, who rescues me when I run out of words and pulls the best from me.

Love to my sons, Spencer and Travis: You are brave guys who have overcome much adversity in your lives and as a result are very wise ahead of your time.

Thanks to my stepfamilies for your love, acceptance and support!

Thanks to Jan Coleman, my editor, who helped me finish my first work and keep focus. You have such creativity and truly live up to your tagline, brilliance on demand.

Thanks to Colleen Foshee, Lisa Ramsey,and Margie Chapman for all your help and understanding in areas I don't have a clue about. I admire your gifts and leadership.

Thanks to our former precious speaking group, who let me discover with them how to express ourselves. Special love to Dorothy Newton and Wendy Saxton for hosting, Colleen for co-leading.

Thanks to ProvenWay Ministries, my sponsor, for support, patience, and guidance.

Thanks to Phyllis Jenkins and Powerful Journey for giving me opportunity to speak. You really do help women flourish.

Thanks to Marshawn Evans for inspiration.

Thanks to Janet Uszynski and Orchid for believing in me and giving me practice.

Thanks to Gateway Church for outstanding leadership equipping and wonderful conferences like *Pink Impact*.

Thanks to NTCW and Lena Nelson Dooley and Lee Carver and gang for help in writing.

Thanks to Ellen Foehner and Lori Lazzeri for all your mentoring help, prayer and listening ear.

Thanks to VJ Photography for photo on back cover.

Thanks to Chris Schell for cover design.

Thanks to Stephanie Adams, my niece, for your expertise in overseeing the publishing. Love you!

Holly W. Smith

TABLE OF CONTENTS

FOREWORD

God has embedded within the spiritual DNA of each person the potential to maximize their spiritual effectiveness. He has uniquely created us, mind, body, soul and spirit to impact for Christ the habitat we occupy. (Acts 17:26) He has similarly given us gifts to aid in the accomplishment of our primary calling; expanding the Kingdom of God in our midst.

We are able, as citizens of the Kingdom, to integrate both our successes and failures, our lapses of obedience and our moments of whole hearted devotion into a cohesive testimony which magnifies the goodness, majesty and love of God. There is no calamity or transgression which does not contain within it the seeds of redemption, for the Christian.

No other pursuit in life has this magnificent potential. There are no other arenas in life where broken and powerless creatures can alter the course of human history, carrying the glory and majesty of the Creator in containers of clay. Each of us has a unique platform, an audience we alone can impact, a calling which can't be replicated.

Don't let the enemy steal this perspective-there is no substitute for *you*.

Alan Smith

PREFACE

This book came into being after sharing my story at the Powerful Journey conference last February at Hope Center in Plano, Texas. Women came up to say they wanted to hear more. They wanted to think about the lessons and read the book. There was no book. So I went home, fresh from the seminar, and wrote the story I had spoken. I wanted to give more as they asked so I added some background, experiences with women, and more detail about the dream of my mission I sought for over twenty years. Though at first I didn't understand the symbols in dreams, I feel so blessed that God speaks to me in that manner. The thrill of a vision that is vivid and touches your heart can *never* be taken from you. I want to give hope to other women that God is faithful to keep His promises. Thanks for encouraging me to write.

Holly W. Smith

No eye has seen, no ear has heard, no mind has conceived what God has prepared for those who love Him but God has revealed it to us by His Spirit. (1 Cor. 2:9)

INTRODUCTION

I would be remiss not to reveal the real source and root of my childhood insecurities. I was born with several benign tumors and a birthmark on my upper legs which caused the coloration of my skin in that area to be slightly darker. The growths necessitated surgical removal and skin grafts, to eliminate any possibility of future danger. Because of my young age and the fact that I was still crawling, my legs didn't heal properly and scarred. I was very self-conscious as a result and attempted to conceal my scars.

I was raised as a Christian, attending the Baptist church. I believed in Jesus at an early age, although I envisioned him to be more like Santa, dispensing extraordinary gifts to children who had been good. I became interested in the miracles Jesus performed, hoping to secure my own. I reasoned that Hayley Mills, or other child stars had no such defect and I aspired to be like one of them. Every night I prayed for a restoration of the skin on my body, so that it would be like my brother or sister's. I would wake each morning and peer under the covers to inspect my legs, fully expecting to be miraculously transformed overnight. My hopes were repeatedly dashed, though I sincerely believed one morning would be different. I remember questioning: Do miracles exist *today*? That's the kind of God I wanted. Evidently, this wasn't the kind of miracle He planned for me.

My cosmetic defect produced a seed of comparison, which grew like a weed in the garden of my self-confidence. While waiting for a miracle to manifest, I was in a state of constant comparison, imagining smooth skin to be the source of all joy in my universe and a new emerging future. Additionally, after opening the door to this diseased thinking, I complicated the issue, attempting to emulate the scholastic achievement of my sister, who incidentally graduated with high honors from SMU Law School. My feeble attempts to copy her ended up like Custer at the Little Bighorn.

I was a happy child, despite all this and felt loved and protected in my family. Nevertheless, the public swimming pool often became a place of shame, as my secret source of disappointment was apparent to all.

I want to encourage those who have a true handicap to know God loves you and has a plan to integrate your personal struggle into a solution and source of inspiration for others. This is the essence of Christianity; overcoming difficulty through faith, patience and the work of His spirit.

Later in life, I learned to fully embrace my flaws and reality. I found *Holly* again! I am grateful that God led me to reinterpret the priorities of life, replacing my shame with a desire to cause others to recapture their hope and purpose. Actually, I learned to see life differently, as a result of abandoning the superficial perspective I had as a child. The very thing that disqualified me from acceptance by the world and contentment as a child, qualified me for adult ministry. As I aged, I began to authentically identify with the pains and shortcomings of others. I am glad God was patient with me and caused me to see the truth of my circumstances. I prefer it to the vain, self-centered existence I might have embraced, had He not revealed His higher purposes in allowing me to endure my personal trials.

You may erroneously believe that the removal of obstacles and conquest of your circumstances is the key to happiness and achievement. That is a lie. The recapture of your true identity is the only source of "peace that passes all understanding", and can only be achieved, as you conquer your attitude and overcome evil with good. You are a lighthouse with a unique beacon, which draws only those whom God has selected to your signal.

I eventually married and my husband and I began attending a spirit filled church in Arlington, Texas. This congregation embraced a belief in the supernatural, which energized my zeal for service in a new and exciting manner. As a result, I began bombarding God with prayer, night and day to reveal his purposes in my life, as well as my personal gifts. One night I had a dream, which featured the following words printed on a banner: HOUSECLEANERS OVER THE LORD'S HOUSE, WATCHER OVER THE WORD. I identified the watcher segment as belonging to my husband, as he always harbored a preoccupation with the timing and specific detail of God's activity in the earth. I didn't know what to think of the housecleaner part. Wasn't sure if I wanted to be a housekeeper.

I later understood the essence of this revelation: to provide a ministry of comfort to others, as I allowed them to rid themselves of emotional and spiritual toxins. I was also aware of their need to re-consecrate themselves, following an extended season of difficulty, counseling or alienation from the faith. I had to endure an extended season of trial, renewal and consecration myself however, before I would be rescuing anybody else.

I later dreamed my purse had glue in it, which I interpreted to be empowerment to connect women together through friendship and introduction. I love helping people.

Here is my story.

CHAPTER ONE

Degree or Decree?

I will give you a new heart and put a new spirit in you. I will remove from you your heart of stone and give you a heart of flesh. And I will put my Spirit in you and move you to follow my decrees.
Ezekiel 36:26-27

We all experience dreams, probably thousands in our lifetime. Most of them aren't very significant and are soon forgotten. But have you ever had one that wouldn't let you go? A dream so powerful that it made you wonder if it was a message from God? I had one of those dreams. A girlfriend who attended my graduation said to me, "I wish I had received my Master's *decree.*"

Was it a slip of the tongue? Did she mean to say degree? No, it was perfectly clear. She said the word *decree*.

I kept asking myself, what did this dream mean? In the Bible we read that a decree means God's eternal purpose. Have I graduated from some school of spiritual education, I wondered? Have I finally followed God's path and let go of my grandiose plans? Have I come to the place of finally desiring His plans over my own?

My perplexing questions continued. Why had this particular friend said this to me? What was she yearning for that she didn't have? She was a devout Christian woman, but I watched her pursue a conventional path—the widely acceptable way of material acquisition, reputation, and success in the world. Why had she suddenly changed her mind about her direction?

I pondered the dream for a long time. I had come a long way from claiming that my abilities and qualifications were essential to empower me. So what was its message in my life? Did it mean I was heading the right way, on the right path? Maybe I don't need to collect a drawer full of degrees to receive my Master's decree?

A degree is a tangible symbol signifying approval, distinction, or honor. A Master's decree, on the other hand, is a foreordained plan and guidance by a spiritual authority. One requires intellectual pursuit; the other obedience to an invisible faith and kingdom. At last, am I following this invisible path to my destiny? I didn't know the answer to any of these questions, but, in time they would unfold.

What God made known to me, I'm sharing with you.

CHAPTER TWO

Competent Family: What About Me?

Now to each one the manifestation of the Spirit is given for the common good. I Corinthians 12:7

For so long I struggled with the mystery of who I was meant to be. There was a battle going on in my life between worldly and spiritual standards. Yes, I knew the blessings of pursuing godliness, but somehow getting ahead, pursuing success and material things *seemed* more important in the world.

It's a trap so many of us fall into. It reminds me of tumbling into quicksand. You may have seen it in the movies. On the surface quicksand looks like harmless wet soil, but once you're caught in it, you see that it's a bottomless pit that threatens to suck you down under.

Since childhood I wrestled with my identity and rejection issues. I was the middle child in a very competent family. My father was a bank president, my mom a college professor, my brother a star athlete, and my sister a lawyer and senior executive of her company. It was an uphill fight to find my place among such achievers. What do you do when you feel insecure, deeply flawed and inadequate? That's right—you naturally look for affirmation elsewhere. So that's what I did.

Most of us want to be significant, make our mark in the world. We search for our strengths, but often there is no compass or person to guide us, so we flounder. I did make the cheerleading squad, I was a good athlete, but merely an average learner. I was not the *most* excellent in anything.

And excellent is what I strove to be.

Sly and the Family Stone came out with a song years ago called "Everybody is a Star". Is it true, I wondered? The lyrics struck me. Everybody wants to be a star and shine. Yes, we all want to be loved for who we *are* and not for who we think we *need* to be.

Who wouldn't want to believe that?

My elementary teachers hinted at some of my talents. My third grade teacher told me I had a spiritual gift when I gave an oral report about the Easter story. When my parents came to my open house in fourth grade, Mrs. Arthur told them I would be a poet and author.

"She'll have to practice this gift and develop her craft," she said. Her acknowledgement gave me hope that someone in authority recognized ability in me. I was creative and could write a good story, but my form and organization lacked polish, to say the least. My mom had to step in and edit to bring my ideas to final form to turn in.

So I never learned how to complete assignments myself. Writing seemed too time consuming, I thought. Grind out words and write paragraphs over and over again? I was certain I didn't have the self-discipline or patience for that.

Like many of us in our microwave society, I wanted instant gratification. Perfect scores must be the goal. Scholarly achievements seemed to work for my sister, Joni. Since I craved recognition in my family, I decided I must pattern myself after her. After all, kids in the same family turn out identically, don't they? My own insecurities and lack of knowledge led me down a distracting path.

By now, I had a full blown inferiority complex. Each year as I came into my elementary class, the teachers would be delighted when they learned I was Joni's sister. They had high expectations that were soon dashed.

More recently, when we held an eightieth birthday party for my dad, his friends came up and asked, "Are you the one? Are you the one who is a lawyer and owns a home in Napa Valley?"

I would shrug with a cute little wink of the eye and say, "No, I'm not the one."

"Are you the one?" is a classic line in the movie, *The Matrix*, derived from Matthew 11:3. One of the characters, Neo, wants to discover if he is the one to save his kingdom from destruction. Morpheus, much like John the Baptist of the

Bible, has been looking to prepare the way for the one to come. When he meets Neo, he believes he's found the rescuer. Then Neo is sent to the oracle to find out his destiny. The oracle tells Neo he is very gifted but not the *one*.

The oracle didn't tell the truth, but it was what he needed to hear at that moment in time.

Later, he discovers he *is* the *one*. He rises to his greatness when he chooses to risk his life for Morpheus and is given supernatural power to defeat his enemies.

In a similar manner, God often calls us to lay down our lives for them. I wonder if there could be a kingdom where all could qualify by their love. The Bible tells us the disciples were known by their love for each other. Would God back us up with supernatural power as He had Neo?

In the near future, I would be tested on my love for different kinds of people.

I can tell you this by experience, when you doubt God's favor for you the temptation is to turn on your reasoning, engage your mind to figure out a plan, a way to excel and be noticed. I presumed all I needed to be was ...smarter. If only I could understand my math problems better and the jokes my parents and sister told on the way to church. Then I would be accepted.

Since I was two years younger than Joni, I often felt I simply didn't *get* it. My sister would sit between our parents in the front seat on the way to church and giggle about their jokes. My brother was in his own world and didn't mind, probably thinking about his favorite TV show, *Combat*, or GI Joe. I felt terribly left out. You may remember a song by Cat Stevens, "Father to Son." It speaks of a son breaking away from his father, pursuing his own destiny. It talks about the times he cried, keeping all the things he knew inside. No longer can he ignore the feelings that the path for others wouldn't work for him.

I was too young to break away from my parents, but I yearned to pursue my own identity, and yet find a way to fit in and measure up.

One Sunday at church I wrote in pencil on the leaflet:

Dear God, All I want for Christmas is the gift of understanding...

I believe God began to answer that prayer, though not in the way I expected. If I could have heard His voice then, I believe He would have said,

Holly, I want you to understand my kingdom. I want you to know my values, what success means to me; standing in the shoes of others, comforting others with the comfort I'll

give you, having compassion. I want you to know that I've made the foolish to shame the wise, the weak to shame the strong. You can qualify in my kingdom.

How freeing that would have been if I had known that there was another system out there where we only needed to be concerned with pleasing God.

Nevertheless, I continued to compare myself with Joni, and a competitive spirit *grew* within me.

CHAPTER THREE

A New Paradigm

For since there is jealousy and quarreling among you, are you not worldly? Are you not acting like mere men? I Corinthians 3:3

Have you ever compared yourself with another? Envied someone for what they had that you didn't? We are born into this environment admiring the best musician, star athlete, most beautiful model or actress. As kids we model ourselves after them. It's a natural part of growing up, but if we have unrealistic expectations like being the next winner on *American Idol*, we can be crushed when we fail.

Like me you may feel you got the short end of the stick in your genetic pool. It's so easy to guess what God should have done, how He could have made us different and better. I can be president of that club. We all have the same mantra; if only He had created us this way or that, we could *really* have been something.

In waltzes regret for what could have been. Out goes living in the present and appreciating what we *do* have.

Envy is desiring something someone else has. Jealousy is being afraid of losing what you already have. I was guilty of both. I wanted Joni's brains and feared losing my parent's attention and favor. It didn't stop with Joni. I began to compare myself with everyone who was more capable and had a better situation than my own. I didn't know the plan I was devising was really of selfish ambition, trying to create and achieve my own significance. It's such a snare, but we can learn to recognize the signs and differences:

WORLD'S WAY /	*GOD'S KINGDOM*
Selfish ambition-striving to get own needs met, following own desires	*God meets needs, following God's will*
Pride	*Humility*
Self-sufficient	*Dependent on God*
Self-seeking, idol of self, control	*Self-sacrifice, prefer another, surrender*

Take all you need	*Give and it will be given to you*
Climb success ladder	*First will be last, humble exalted*
Look after own interests	*Look into the interests of others*
Faith in own ability, strengths	*Faith in God's ability to act through us*
Hope in advancing self	*Hope to advance God in others' lives*
Quarreling, dissension, disorder	*Love neighbor as self*
Competition with fellow man	*Peace, love, harmony*
Immaturity	*Spiritual maturity*
Jealousy, envy	*Rejoice with those who rejoice*
Defined by achievements	*Defined by character*
Most capable	*When weak, He is strong*
Most beautiful	*God looks at the heart*
Live for applause of men	*Audience of One*

Curse	*Bless when cursed*
Looking for rewards, riches	*More blessed to give than receive*
Strong urge to achieve	*Carry each other's burdens*
Use gifts to advance popularity	*Use gifts to serve others*

CHAPTER FOUR

Confessions of a Green-eyed Girl

Do not judge, or you too will be judged. Matthew 7:1

Comparison creates jealousy. It's a thief that keeps us from fulfilling our own mission. It also may lead to other wrong behaviors. God began showing me that I was judging wrongly. Trying to size up my opponent is a very unhealthy way of thinking. Once I fell into the competitive spirit, I would evaluate my adversary and see something critical. This evaluation always made me feel better about myself. She is not *that* great of a mother. She's not as *thin* as I am. She's not *that* cute...

I had a girlfriend once who seemed a bit cold. As far as sharing transparently or any intimate details of her life, she was shut down. But I liked her a lot and decided the feeling was mutual. I emailed her often, sharing somewhat deep things because I'm not one for too much shallow talk.

She wouldn't respond right away, sometimes up to several weeks. I felt very rejected. As this cycle continued, I finally came to the conclusion that this wasn't about me. There must be something so painful in her life that she couldn't face talking about anything serious.

It dawned on me that I judged her behavior because of my hurt that she didn't respond to my authentic sharing in the way I expected. Yes, I expected her to be just like me, to open up as I had, and when she didn't I began to resent her. I confessed to the Lord that I was sorry. I vowed to love her just as she is. She reached out the best way she knew how. After I made this confession to God, something amazing happened. The next time I heard from her she talked more openly and deeply than ever.

God showed me a tangible difference. When I let go of my judgmental attitude—that kept the process in perpetual motion—He answered my prayer for my friend by prompting her to open up. As long as I hung onto this pattern of criticizing others for not living up to my expectations, I was stuck in it.

Another way we fall into errors in our thinking is judging by outward appearance. I assumed a certain leader —a few years older than me—was out-of-date and way behind me spiritually. How proud was that? Why, she even boasted at times about her accomplishments. The Lord again showed me how to see into her heart, and she proved to be as loving as my own grandmother and more helpful with the tasks I struggled with. As she mentored me I affirmed her, and what a difference it made.

It reminded me that I am a former recovering boasting addict myself. Boasting is a sign of insecurity. I should be able to overlook some of these things and see the good in others if I want people to overlook my humanity as well.

Another way we compete in our outward appearance is striving to be the most *fair* in the land. We generally think of movie stars in this category. You'd think they would be on top of the world with their beauty and fame, but they can be the most insecure and messed up people on the planet. What happens when that fountain of youth runs out?

The first thing we notice about a person is her appearance but someone can have a pretty face and yet be an empty shell of a person. When someone is totally relying on their looks, they don't work on the substance of who they *truly* are. Think of someone you knew in high school or now whom you really know as a total person. Their warmth, personality, and spirit make them beautiful in your eyes. Someone else may meet them and not see their beauty at all because they haven't gotten to know their character as you do. I am reminded of an old ballad by Santana called, "She's not There". It was a song about a guy who got his heart broken by a girl who was a fake. He talks about how no one told him about her and how she lied. Still he had to recall how glamorous she looked, and how she acted, her hair, voice, and eyes but *she's not there...* In other words, he was duped by the facade of her beauty.

We must build our lives on something more.

One day while working out at the gym I met a girl who was selling a huge quantity of her clothes. We were about the same size, though she was about ten years younger and a hairdresser. Naturally I wanted to come over and try on a few outfits, but when I began I noticed that each one was a bit racy; a low neck, a plunging back, super short skirt. Nothing I would take home, for sure. Maybe she was in a certain phase in her life, I thought, where she needed to feel feminine and sexy, that she still had it, that sexual appeal to attract others.

I was there once, needing approval from my appearance, but over time my thinking matured. It didn't seem necessary to dress like that anymore. Thank goodness. It made me grateful that I had grown out of this stage, and there was more to me now. I bought a few T-shirts and left.

CHAPTER FIVE

Divine Guidance

And I will ask the Father, and He will give you another Counselor to be with you forever—the Spirit of truth. John 14:16

My mom was a strong influence in my life. She sent me a book in college called *Search for Significance*. It is now an old classic by Robert McGee that rings true. The vacuum and emptiness we all feel inside can only be filled by Christ. Our search for meaning and significance points back to who we are in Him. This lesson from Robert McGee showed me once again that security is only found in Him. If I could just keep that focus. My thoughts kept returning to my shortcomings that disqualified me from succeeding and who I should be.

After graduating from University of Texas at Austin in Physical Education and Health, I decided to do something different for a few years before teaching.

I became a flight attendant for Braniff International Airlines and moved to Denver, Colorado. I met a friend, Lori, working a flight. Lori radiated light and a calm manner of diligence. She displayed something I wanted and lacked. We became friends on our layover and decided to meet for lunch in Denver. I found out the reason for her confidence. She was a reborn Christian. She seemed so assured and anchored in her faith. She consulted God for guidance about her affairs. I was a Christian but didn't have that kind of relationship. I wanted more. I was so hungry and drawn to His presence in her that she could hardly stay a day ahead with my questions, she tells me now.

Lori brought me some books. One was *The Cross and the Switchblade* by David Wilkerson. It was about Nicky Cruz, the teen gang member whose life was transformed by David Wilkerson's ministry. The other book was *The Holy Spirit and You* by Dennis Bennett. This book related how to receive the Holy Spirit.

Both these books ministered to me as I felt guilt over a bit of a wild past my insecurities had driven me to. I didn't know how God would accept me again. However, when I saw how God anointed this young man, Nicky, who had even murdered someone, I knew God's grace could cover me also. After receiving the Holy Spirit in his life, Nicky helped thousands of teens and gang members be saved and delivered from their lifestyle. The Holy Spirit empowered him and made him *more* effective.

Lori and I visited a church called *Vineyard Christian Fellowship* in the foothills. Fred Stipes was the minister. When the congregation began singing the worship songs, I noticed some were raising their hands, others had tears streaming down their faces. I sensed God's presence and the sincere hearts in this congregation.

Church had been pretty boring up to this time for me. I usually patted myself on the head for going but the sermon lesson didn't make a lasting impression. Often if someone asked, I could not even recall the subject or passage studied. This service was different. The illustration of an ice skater who kept persevering in practice and the application to my own life took new wings. The message penetrated and lasted the whole week until I could get another drink from this deep well of refreshment the next Sunday.

Lori and I planned a trip to Cancun. We both needed a vacation and that was the beauty of the benefit of our flight pass privileges. It made up for the low salary at that time. We left in the middle of a winter blizzard in Denver. We arrived that afternoon in Cancun and unpacked into our little bungalow on the beach. We had a restful time reading and soaking up sunshine. After dinner, I asked Lori to pray for me to receive the Holy Spirit. As she prayed, I felt a stirring in my spirit, a warmth like a hug for a few minutes and I heard a still small voice saying,

You don't need anything to numb your pain. You only need Me.

I knew I had made a deeper commitment to God and enjoyed this new intimacy. I experienced a sweet prayer time like never before. Maybe I would now receive guidance as Lori does. I was almost twenty-four and a new chapter was opening in my life. I had hope out of the chaos I felt previously.

After a few years in Colorado, I missed Texas and my family. I transferred back to the Braniff base in the Dallas Fort Worth area. I broke up with my boyfriend, Bob, who didn't understand praying about every decision in my newfound faith. I knew I couldn't trust my own way anymore.

I got my residential real estate license in Arlington and sold houses on the side between my flights with Braniff. A real estate friend in the office set me up on a blind date with a partner of his in commercial real estate. We went out to dinner at Japanese Palace in Ft. Worth with Roger and his girlfriend, Mary. They had told us before the date that we would be perfect for each other.

"You both jog and care about fitness." They didn't know how to say we both were Christians and attended church. They only said we had a lot in common. They were right. The chemistry between us was perfect. We saw each other for the next solid month nightly. We were married two months later. I was twenty-seven and Alan twenty-nine.

CHAPTER SIX

Mend Fences

For you shall know the truth and the truth shall set you free. John 8:32

Our two sons came in swift succession. I discovered for the first time what *busy* really means. If you've had toddlers, you know what I'm saying. I began attending Bible Study Fellowship. I remember being inspired by our study of John and the passage for the week, John 8:32, *For you shall know the truth and the truth shall set you free.*

Before one of the Wednesday morning sessions, I went jogging around the neighborhood. My prayers turned into venting.

"Oh, Lord, my life has not turned out like I planned. My husband has some anger issues I didn't know about when we married. I have these two boys in a row that are a handful, my parents are divorced, and I am depressed. I wonder—what is the truth for *me* and how will it set *me* free?"

As I pondered the scripture, *For you shall know the truth and the truth shall make you free,* I asked this question over and over again. Suddenly I felt an impression and a voice inside my heart.

Holly, I want to bless you but you must take responsibility for your actions. You need to go and get rid of all your offenses, otherwise they will build up like a huge snowball gaining momentum and become too burdensome to carry. Do you remember the fairy tale, Sleeping Beauty? When the child was born, the fairy godmothers gave their blessing. Then the wicked witch gave her curse and plan for destruction.

I want to give my blessing but harboring a spirit of unforgiveness is the enemy's plan to curse and destroy you.

Even if your offense resulted from an unfair hurt by another, do your part in confessing your resentment and putting the ordeal back in the other's court to deal with. In this way you will take back the territory the enemy has stolen from you and come into my blessings. I will be with you...

Gulp, okay. Did the God of the universe just speak to me? Yes, I believe He gave me a *decree*. I thought it so personal for God to relate a childhood tale to illustrate the battle going on for our blessing or downfall. He seemed to talk in my own language.

At home I made a list of people toward whom I felt resentment. First, let me say that there wasn't a mean bone in my body. I wanted to be liked, accepted, and get attention. I would not purposely be mean or aggressive for any reason. But when people had taken advantage of *me*, run over *me*, rejected *me*, *then* I had taken up an offense and resented them for hurting me unjustly.

Over the next few weeks I met with some people on my list, called or left a note for others, and tried to clear my part of any problems. Certainly I wouldn't hear from some nor get apologies back, but I wasn't to be concerned with that.

There was a particular girl in my neighborhood that I especially admired. Okay, *envied.* Melanie was married to a doctor, had a larger home than mine, and a glamorous one at that. Her kids were always dressed and groomed perfectly. I envied her and secretly longed to change places with her. Not to have her husband, of course, but her situation and the way she seemed to manage her life. I wrote a note expressing my admiration for her. I admitted that, as a Christian, I had crossed a line in envying her life. I apologized and conveyed a blessing to her and her family. That was it.

I didn't hear back from her.

Oops, my rejection button was pushed. Humbled and embarrassed, I reminded myself that it was what God had asked me to do. He had given me the *decree*. I was responsible to be obedient and leave the outcome to Him.

A few months later, my Bible study held an Orientation day for women to visit and decide if they would like to attend. I asked four ladies in the neighborhood, and they all consented to come, including Melanie, who joined the study. By the end of the semester she had recommitted her life and her whole family to the Lord. Not only did she become active in her church, she became the choir director.

And she ended up thanking me for encouraging her in coming back to the Lord.

I don't tell this story to put a notch in my belt—though I like notches as well as anybody—but to show that when we follow our Master's *decree* and humble ourselves, God opens up doors of opportunity. I merely followed the prompt of my heart that allowed God to *woo* her back to Himself. He began to show me the fruit of following His way.

Let's give Him applause! Yay God!

As far as I knew I had completed my task, reconciled with the people on my list. It didn't dawn on me that the list must include my sister.

Oops. I had left her name off. I loved Joni dearly, but I was at odds at how to reconcile with her. What I didn't know was that you cannot really love someone wholeheartedly when you're still in competition with them.

CHAPTER SEVEN

Does God Still Speak?

They said to him, We have had dreams, and there is no one to interpret them. And Joseph said to them, Do not interpretations belong to God? Please tell them to me. Genesis 40:8

Alan and I began to go to counseling. It was time that we faced up to the fact that our marriage wasn't what it should be. Counseling proved painful. We both had a lot of issues we had brought into our marriage, but we both had the desire to change and make the way better for our children. We did not want them to inherit problems and fears but God's promises.

Travis, Holly, and Spencer

God began orchestrating dreams to springboard the healing process. I had always had vivid dreams as a child. Stan, our counselor, said we can appreciate them as a *gift* and write them down to ponder their meanings. A passage in Job 33 verifies that God *does* speak though we don't always perceive it. He speaks through His word, through nature, even through a movie that touches a chord. This passage says He may speak in a dream or vision in the night. He may warn us to keep us from doing wrong, preserve us from danger, or keep us from pride. Hebrews 13:8 reminds us that *Jesus is the same yesterday, today and forever*. I knew God used dreams frequently in Biblical times. I just didn't know He was still using them today.

At *least* with *me*.

We all hear from God. Not everyone hears a message from God in a dream, but some do. We prayerfully examine the Word of God and make sure our dreams are in agreement with Scripture. If so, we must also consider what God would have us do in response to our dream. God always makes the meaning of the dream clear. (James 1:5)

It's important to ask Him what He is trying to communicate to you through the dream or strong impression. Stan told us to bring our dreams to each session, and he would help us interpret them. Since Stan is a pastor and a psychologist, I trusted him to help us recognize God's intentions through the images and symbols. The following week I brought him my dream. It portrayed a gift my sister, Joni, and I were giving our mom. Joni's gift was a beautiful, colorful vase. It was perfect. My gift to Mom was a dull, cracked pot.

That's right, a *cracked pot*.

I had an inkling of what it meant, but the counselor helped clarify the meaning for me. Joni's offering represented the perfect, capable, achieving daughter; mine was the flawed, marred, deficient one. Each represented us and a side of our mother: the competent and the frailty common with all humanity.

Okay, *wait* just a minute here. We may all be a bit broken but do I have to be reminded that I can't quite measure up? I don't like representing the flawed side of my mom. I doubt she likes relating to me either if it reminds her of her own weakness.

I found myself mad at God again. He knew how insecure and inadequate I already felt. Why would He continue to rub it in confirming my ineptness, and make me feel worse about myself?

CHAPTER EIGHT

Death of *Good Girl*

All our righteous acts are like filthy rags. Isaiah 64:6

I was still trying to perfect myself and be a *good girl* at that time. I thought I had been a pretty good wife; obedient, spent time in the Word, spent time in prayer just that morning. The week had been a victorious one, and here I was falling into the condemnation pit again. This imperfection was no fun and an impossible label to shake.

Then God began to show me something interesting.

There is something to this *good girl* label. It's a stereotype for women. "Boys will be boys," but girls are expected to be good and kind. I'm sure it causes women to suppress their true feelings at times. Most women hate conflict or talking directly to someone about differences. If we think we must be good no matter what, what do we do with our feelings? We *stuff* them.

We stay silent and tell ourselves we're doing the right thing.

God had given me a mandate, a personal directive. Resolve your differences. How can the truth set us free if we can't look others in the eye honestly, with graciousness, refusing to allow grudges to grow? It's actually hypocritical to stuff our feelings until they turn to bitterness.

As John Ortberg says in his book, *Everybody's Normal Till You Get to Know Them*, "Bitterness is like drinking rat poison...and waiting for the rat to die."

Once, I avoided being completely honest with a friend, Julia. I didn't want to risk losing her friendship. So I simply avoided confrontation on an issue, choosing instead to bury it, assuming unconditional love could preserve the relationship. It didn't. I soon discovered that only the truth would save what we had.

Julia called me on it. Fortunately, she had the courage to point out something false in me. Oh, it hurt, but it's the kind of hurt that heals. I kept telling myself it was godly to overlook things that bothered me. Once I removed the mask and shared my true feelings, it cleared the air and led us to a deeper intimacy with one another. Hashing things out propels us forward.

Coming clean helps us come unstuck. Being honest will set us free to love more fully.

Two diverse messages have been dominating forces in my life. One stems from the traditions of man in our way of interaction; the other is the Word of God which commands us to *put off* falsehood and *be* truthful.

I walked a shaky tightrope between the two.

One day Alan asked me if I heard anything from God during my prayer time while out running. Often he would come back from his jogs with impressions, words, and scriptures. He would take off writing a page at a time, swept up into prose that seemed wonderfully swift and effortless. My competitive spirit reared its head again. The more I tried to hear, the less I heard. Asking me these questions made me want to "produce," to compete with him, to share my great revelations, even if I had to invent them.

My frustration limit arrived one morning during my run when I started venting yet again:

"I don't understand you, God. I have been out there throwing the football to the boys, taking them to practice, making dinner while Alan is lying across the bed complaining of a sinus infection. When I am doing all these things, why are you pouring out your words to him and not me? I have wanted to hear from you and haven't heard anything lately."

Silence, and then I sensed His answer:

Your righteousness is filthy rags to me. At least Alan knows he is a sinner and depends on me for his righteousness...

Oops, there it is again. There is no one good but Jesus. Why am I trying so hard? Why can't I get it through my head that Jesus became sin for us that we might become righteous through Him. Even Paul said, I don't do what I want to do. "What a wretched man I am!" Perhaps that's why salvation is a gift so no one can boast about earning it.

Even though it was a rebuke, I welcomed it. It proved I was growing.

CHAPTER NINE

"Houston, We Have a Problem!"

It is the glory of God to conceal a matter; to search out a matter is the glory of kings. Proverbs 25:2

A few months later after my dream of the cracked pot, I attended a *Big Sister's Benefit*. Big Sister is an amazing national organization whose mission is to help girls realize their potential through positive mentoring relationships with women. In the back of the auditorium were prizes for the big drawing, so I scanned them to see what my ticket might win for me. When I spotted a beautiful painting in my favorite Santa Fe motif my jaw dropped. It was an image of a cracked pot, the same cracked pot in my dream.

And then the unimaginable happened. When the ticket was drawn to win this painting, it was mine! This was no mere coincidence. I became the new owner of this, $1000 painting.

How could I not take the cracked pot message seriously? Again, what did it mean? That

I am the cracked pot? I was amazed at the confirmation.

Big Sister's Benefit Prize

I turned to the Bible. God knows we will struggle with some of these mysteries, and I vowed to search out all the clay and pot scriptures to bring more illumination. The next step is to study Bible characters who also struggled with comparison issues. Surely there are examples and illustrations of how to handle some of these questions.

The first scripture revealed to me was Psalm 51:17, *The sacrifices of God are a broken spirit; a broken and contrite heart, He will not despise.*

There is something about being contrite, humble, and broken that God esteems.

The theme of the potter and clay is an awesome picture of the sovereignty of God, of His loving and sovereign hand over all our affairs. His desire is to mold and shape broken men and women.

In 2 Corinthians 4:7 (NLT) we are reminded that we are like fragile clay jars containing great treasure. We're flawed vessels so that the power may be from God and not us. My study Bible footnotes explain that in the old days the Jews clay pots were not at all decorative, but cheap, common pots. They were so ordinary they attracted no attention whatsoever. So what did the Jews do? Hide their treasure in them because nobody would ever suspect there was something valuable inside.

What a beautiful illustration of us, plain and ordinary on the outside but with the magnificent power of the Holy Spirit on the inside. In fact when the apostle Paul is accused of being weak and simple he replies by saying, "Absolutely. I'm a clay pot, but God uses clay pots so that the power may be from God and not ourselves."

The Scriptures tell us that the potter has the right over the clay, to take it and create what He wishes. He chose some pots for special purposes and some for common use. As I pondered this I realized: I must be made for common use?

It's interesting how the clay, in Romans 9 and Isaiah 45, actually questions the potter. The clay asks: "Why did you make me like this?" Isn't that a familiar cry of our hearts? Have you ever argued with God about this? For me the answer is obvious—many times over. I never appreciated *the way* He made me; common, ordinary, flawed, nothing to brag about.

Or so I thought.

Why wasn't I smarter, prettier I often lamented? Bitter complaints crossed my mind many times. But the potter answers the clay,

"No, don't say that. Who are you, a mere human being, to argue with God? Should the thing that was created complain to the one who created it?" (Romans 9:29) He is basically saying: Aren't you turning things upside down as if you were the boss? Doesn't the potter have the right to make out of the same lump of clay some pottery for special uses and some for common use?

God alone has the vision and skill to work with the clay, to smooth out the imperfections.

We are treasures in jars of clay. There may be nothing out of the ordinary about us, nothing spectacular on the outside, but on the inside—the Holy Spirit empowers and enables us. The beauty is that it isn't up to us to conjure up the way to carry out God's message through the Holy Spirit. He will give us the words to speak.

Once I thought you had to be born with the innate ability to speak or write and if it wasn't part of your DNA, tough luck. Now I realize that if God calls you to do something, He will enable you to do it. We are told in 1 Corinthians 1:5-6 that we don't lack any spiritual gift and have been enriched in every way. It is resident *in* us.

I began yearning for more insight and proceeded to my next plan of study. I wanted to learn about the characters in the Bible caught in comparing themselves with another and coming up short. People who became blinded by their jealousy.

First, there are the brothers of Joseph, Rachel and Leah, Sarai and Hagar, and King Saul with his resentment for young David, whom God had chosen as King of Israel.

"Houston, we have a problem!"

As I dove into it more, I asked myself: what areas did these characters commonly battle? Often it was for favor, possessions, children, husband, more desirable circumstances, or even popularity. This is true for our modern times as well.

Joseph's brothers were afraid of losing favor with their father. Their jealousy drove them to try to kill Joseph and sell him into slavery to get him out of the way, grieving their poor father for many years.

Leah was stuck in a marriage of deception, jealous over her husband's devotion to her sister. Rachel was the more beautiful one and Leah, we are told from the Bible, had weak eyes. I have to wonder if it's from crying too much over her plight.

Sarai and Hagar also were constantly at each other's throats. They were in fierce competition to provide an heir for Abraham. Though Sarai set up the servant girl with her husband, the plan backfired. She banished Hagar out to the desert along with Ishmael to fend for themselves.

King Saul competed with David for popularity. Saul looked royal. He was tall and handsome. He became king at thirty and reigned forty two years. But this king had a disobedient heart and the Lord withdrew His favor from him. After David slew Goliath, Saul overheard the crowds say,

"Saul has slain his thousands and David his ten thousands." What, the king was comparing the mighty king with this reckless youth? That set Saul in motion to his destruction. Instead of concentrating on his royal duties, Saul wasted time chasing David through the hills, trying to kill his rival.

The story of Abraham and Lot in Genesis 13 highlights the conflict between two men choosing land for their herds. The most fertile and fruitful land was not always the best choice for blessing.

It's so easy to assume the greener grass is better than our parched dry turf that needs constant toil. I fell into coveting a lifestyle that seemed greater than my own. Because I viewed myself as the best Christ follower I could possibly be, it didn't seem fair that my husband and I had to downsize and go through hard times financially. How unjust, or so I thought. Certainly, this new and downwardly-mobile lifestyle wasn't here to stay.

As one of the first in our age group of friends to prosper and afford some finer things, we began having one setback after another. We couldn't recapture our former success, no matter how we strove.

Was this loss of wealth bad luck or is God trying to teach me something?

One day during my devotions a scripture jumped off the page.

Levi does not have a portion or inheritance like his brothers; the Lord is his inheritance, as the Lord your God told him. Even though the Levites were given no land, since they had helped

Moses deal with those who worshiped the golden calf, they were set apart for special service to the Lord, carrying the ark and ministering to Him. (Deuteronomy 10:8,9)

A complete peace descended over me. The matter was settled in that moment. This was my promise. No, I was not a Levite but God will provide. He will be my portion, our source. And I also prayed I could carry His presence as these Levites and Lori did.

I began to pray, and the spirit of resentment toward those who had treated us unfairly broke off in me. I was free. Why be jealous or covetous of anyone or anything if the Lord is going to take care of us and bring us into our destiny? Suddenly I saw that I did not need to look to others any longer. Just as the potter designs the clay to suit his purposes, God gave me the exact lessons to prepare me for His plan.

Women definitely compete for attention today. We compete to be pretty and smart, but the only problem is: there is always someone prettier, thinner, smarter, or more talented. Needing to be pretty, to feel desirable *breeds* competition. Looks vanish, as we know. If we don't develop something within our character that speaks louder than our looks we'll never be content.

After reviewing these Biblical personalities, I moved on to study the story of brothers Jacob and Esau, rivals for their father's spiritual inheritance and blessing. I was curious to see if there were any parallels in my own life. Indeed, there were.

Jacob was born grasping the heel of his brother. *Grasping the heel* is a Hebrew idiom for *schemer* and *deceiver*. Jacob was trying to get ahead even in the womb. As Jacob grew up, we see that his mother, Rebekah, favored him, while his father, Isaac, was keen on Esau.

Why do parents favor certain children? I don't think it's intentional, but sometimes a child is more like the parent, similar in personality and interests, so it evolves naturally. Some children don't *click* with a certain parent. Jacob was quiet and introspective. He hung around the tents. Esau was an outdoorsman and loved to hunt for wild game, just like his father. To Isaac, Esau was the *real man*.

Each child is uniquely made. If you have children, understand how they're wired and encourage them in their strengths. Try to appreciate their differences.

Isaac was determined to give Esau the family blessing before his death. The blessing was the right to become head of the family and receive a double portion of the father's inheritance. Rebekah plotted to deceive Isaac and to get the blessing for Jacob. Now Isaac was already going against God's will. The prophecy was given to Rebekah before the birth of her sons stating that Jacob would be the ruling son.

But Rebekah, as we women often do, decided against waiting to see if God would work it out. Esau showed himself to be an immoral and careless man. He was so reckless that he sold half of his inheritance to his brother for a bowl of bean soup.

Not exactly the best choice to become head of the family.

So Rebekah's plan succeeded, temporarily. However, when Esau heard about it, he vowed to kill his brother after his father died. Jacob was forced to flee, and found himself far away in Haran working for his Uncle Laban. His mother had helped him sow the seed of deception, but little did he know that he would be embroiled in a deception that would change his life.

He loved Rachel, but he had to work fourteen years instead of seven to acquire her as his wife. In the meantime, Laban tricked him into first marrying Leah, instead. This delay cost seven years of his life.

Why do we strike out on our own instead of waiting on God? Jacob could have gained his inheritance more quickly with a little patience and trust that the Lord would bring it about in His own time. Rebekah had been told from the twin's birth that "the older would serve the younger." Why then would she feel compelled to take it all in her own hands?

Author Janette Oke says, "Impatience can cause wise people to do foolish things." I can relate to that.

Jacob had time to ponder his past and prepare for his future. He knew that he had wronged his brother, and it most likely haunted him. When he finally left Laban's household with his wives, he heard that Esau was coming towards him with 400 men.

Jacob was afraid he and his family would be killed. He sent them ahead to safety and spent the night alone. Perhaps he wanted to think, to pray. We don't know. But the Bible says he wrestled with a man until daybreak. Jacob pleaded for a blessing from his opponent.

Who was this man? In Genesis 32:30, Jacob says, *I saw God face to face.*

God honors our passion and hunger for our spiritual inheritance, and will meet us where we are. But our motive must be pure.

The angel touched Jacob's hip, crippling him with a limp. This limp served as a reminder to him. You can't gain your spiritual inheritance in your own strength. It is a supernatural gift that *only* God can bestow.

Likewise, we cannot live the Christian life in our own strength either. We must be humbled, our motives must change, and we must cease striving, and receive our limp. Our limp is a constant reminder of our weakness, a call to depend on God to *bring* us to His promise for us.

The angel of God changed Jacob's name to Israel; one who has contended with God and man. God will prevail, God will control. The government for our lives will be on His shoulders (Is. 9:6). That is what God wants to do in each of our lives as we release control and governing to Him.

I pondered Jacob's life and thought about parallels in my own. My whole life I grasped for my sister, Joni's heel. I craved recognition from others, proof that I was equal to her. But I constantly failed. I ran like Jacob, at a fast pace. Why? Because I didn't want to process my feelings of pain, shame, failure and being just average.

But now I understand the danger in competing with someone, that the way to peace is acceptance of who you are and the way the Potter created you. Someone reminded me recently: the only person you should try to be better than, is the person you were yesterday.

CHAPTER TEN

Ministry Ambitions R.I.P.

I tell you the truth, unless a kernel of wheat falls to the ground and dies, it remains only a single seed. But if it dies, it produces many seeds. John 12:24

Most of us want to reach out and help people who are lost and hurting. When we belong to a church, we usually ask ourselves how we can be a blessing to others. Alan and I became involved with our church, Grace Vineyard in Arlington (1984). We led a kinship group, teaching Bible lessons. We received a word in a presbytery one night that we would spend quite a bit of time in Kansas City. This word resonated with us and a neighbor actually dropped off moving boxes on our front porch as a funny twist to our calling. We admired the pastor in KC and he had been instrumental in setting our pastor in place to start a branch of the same type Bible church in our area. I loved the idea of going there and hoped for ministry opportunities. Here was our chance to shine. We accepted the challenge joyously, but soon learned how much in common we have with Moses, Prince of Egypt.

Moses became so distressed at seeing his people suffer as slaves under the Egyptians that when he saw one abusing a Hebrew, he promptly killed him. A thoughtless act, born of his passion to help. But Pharaoh pursued and Moses fled to the desert of Midian, virtually a wilderness, for forty years. He became a simple shepherd until God called him out to deliver his people.

We were soon to be sanctioned to the back side of the wilderness to wait for God's empowerment ourselves.

Our experience reminds me of a story. A young minister from Canada, Gary Lamb, came to visit our church in Arlington. He gave simple illustrations with profound impact. He told of a dream where he sat on a bench at a football game, filled with excitement. "I can help; I can block and tackle and catch the ball," he cried out. "Put me in!"

The coach looked over at him. "No, Gary, you need to sit on the bench awhile." Confused, he did what was asked. He settled in and began to eat popcorn, cheering his team on. With a blanket over his legs to curb the chill, he began to enjoy being a spectator. Suddenly, the coach turned to him, "Now Gary, go in now, we need you."

"But coach, it's okay. I'm good. I'm not sure how I'll do. I'm pretty comfortable just like this."

"Get in there," the coach insisted. "Now, we can work through you."

When Gary demanded to be sent into the game, filled with pride, the coach hesitated. Only when Gary yielded and was a team player, did the coach feel he was ready. I see this pattern throughout the Bible. There is an incubation period from the time you are called—commissioned—until you are sent. Jesus called the twelve disciples, but it was a time before he sent them out and gave them power to do miracles in His name.

Sometimes we have to exhaust the part of ourselves that as believers we are invincible, that we alone are the *answer* to the problem at hand, that our sheer spiritual-muscle power is what it will take to conquer. Though we did our small part in Kansas City, we returned with tail between our legs, humbled, and with many failed expectations. Kansas City proved to be a cemetery for our ministry ambitions.

About that time I received a Scripture from Hosea 2:14-16 which seemed to foretell the next period of time for us. It spoke of taking Israel out into the wilderness to speak *tenderly* to her and to bestow vineyards and fruitfulness back to her. The scripture spoke of turning the present Valley of Achor into a door of hope and opportunity.

After that the Lord would be a husband to Israel not a slave master.

I knew what the Valley of Achor meant, *valley of trouble*. It's a small valley somewhere in the eastern Judean desert, just east of Jericho. The battle of Achor was the only one the Israelites lost in their conquest of the Promised Land. The Israelites could not stand against their enemies because they had not obeyed the instructions for success. Yet Isaiah 65:10 says that one day the Valley of Achor will be a resting place for herds again and for all those who seek God and inquire of Him. So what's the message here? If we go into battle trying to please ourselves without following guidance, we can get defeated. If we set aside ourselves and follow his decrees, we can't lose.

Sometimes the Lord allows us to fail before we see hope. He's trying to accomplish something in our lives, if only we'll listen and yield. He wants to bring us to the point of remembering who we depend on, to seek Him with our whole heart.

We were definitely in the valley of trouble. I banked on its being our door of hope one day just as it was for Israel.

CHAPTER ELEVEN

Lessons from a Mentor

Do not conform to the pattern of this world, but be transformed by the renewing of your mind.
Romans 12:2

My friend and mentor, Bonnie Malone, died of cancer shortly after she turned 43. She taught me a whole new way of seeing things. I wrote a letter of thanks to her for all her wise counsel over the years and preparation for tribulations we face in life.

Dear Bonnie,

I wanted to encourage you with a few thoughts. I went to a women's retreat last weekend and one of the questions we were asked in a small group was who, outside of your family, has made a big impact on your life and why? I chose you because I'll never forget what you taught me through your pain and real life situations.

You taught me about not competing and being grateful for who I am. You taught me to look for what God made me to be and do. You taught me not to resent those who mistreated me but to stand in their shoes and have compassion for them. You said they may even be jealous of me and I was to feel their insecurity that would make me a threat to them.

Most of all, on the other side of a difficulty, disturbance, or suffering and pain was a gift to be grateful for. As we embrace our suffering, it feels like a group of balloons rising to the heavens and it gives way to peace. We are growing in wisdom through these trials. What a different perspective you have given me: to face life and scoop up suffering and pain like it is gold to be put in the bank and write a check on one day.

I don't know when you have been more accurate in praying for strength for me to bear up under the peelings the Lord would bring. He has brought many and continues to peel the layers. I had adapted many old patterns from well meaning teachers and leaders but they were wrong models.

When the curtain is pulled back, we see ourselves, things we've never seen before. I wonder how God had grace and patience with me in my dysfunction. It gives me more understanding and patience for others.

Funny that my idea of drawing closer to Him would be in the area of greater love and moving more by His spirit. His idea has been to crush some areas of my life so that I wouldn't and absolutely couldn't depend on myself anymore. I wouldn't take a million for this experience or give a plug nickel for another!

I'm at a loss to tell others about it but they must know that they will never be the same... I guess that is good because we need a whole new foundation for new kingdom paradigms. I am reminded of a scripture in Psalms 147:10 that says God's pleasure is not in the strength of the horse or His delight in the legs of a man; but He delights in those who fear Him and put their trust in His unfailing love. He's not impressed with my capabilities or resources but my reliance on Him.

I'm grateful for all your wisdom and advice to prepare me to live my life in God's economy. God bless you and your family. I am praying for your healing and comfort.

Love,

Holly

CHAPTER TWELVE

Character Chiseling

Train a child in the way he should go, and when he is old he will not turn from it. Proverbs 22:6

As a result of our great adventure for God in Kansas City, we were forced to scale down our lifestyle. Most of it didn't bother me, but sharing a car, now that proved the biggest challenge. I felt convicted to homeschool our sons, to pass on God's values to them. I admit to you; I didn't enter into this season graciously nor function triumphantly. First, organization is not my strong suit. The discipline to teach and regulate a classroom day, along with lesson planning and grading, proved more difficult than I imagined. As I saw neighborhood children heading off to the school bus clutching their lunch boxes, I felt a bit of longing. So much for lunch dates with girlfriends or fun shopping trips.

In that day, homeschooling was so unacceptable you had to keep your kids in the house until after 3 p.m. so the truant officer couldn't spot you.

Whenever you try to impart God's wisdom to your children, you know God is working on your character. Children want to see their parents "walk their talk," live out the Bible lessons they teach.

During those years, I hosted a ladies' Bible study in my house. On the heels of losing one of our friends, Laura, I customized a short study from the book of Luke, and I discovered a knack for challenging believers to see God's hands in everything. Laura's dying request had been for Kathy to attend Bible study, though she had worked many years with no chance to do it. Trice had been a friend since fourth grade. Having sociability with other adults, Trice and Kathy, helped with my confinement more than you know.

On Fridays my dad came by and took me to Luby's Cafeteria for a much needed break. Still, at the end of the day, I dismissed myself to my prayer closet to talk with God.

What happened to the promise and blessing You had for me? I feel like I am jumping out of my skin. You know, I'm not used to sitting still. This time with the boys is a good work, but do You remember how I wanted to do great exploits for You and make my mark? I thought You promised...

Lord, this confining time made me contemplate my past and think about my future. I realize and confess that I have sometimes made my husband and kids idols, placing them before You. I wanted their love and acceptance so desperately. In fact, I have even put my mission before my relationship with You sometimes. I repent for that also. Oh yes, I sometimes boast about my own accomplishments, needing affirmation and approval so badly.

Well somebody had to...(smile)

Bottom line, it came to me that my cup was still not full from my childhood. I was still half empty from the attention I longed for, especially when I compared myself to my sister Joni.

But I do know now, God, that Your grace is sufficient for me. Your word says Your power is made perfect in our weakness and that we should only boast about our weaknesses so that Your power might rest on us. That's what I want Lord; Your power, and to be concerned with Your reputation, not my own. I just want a relationship with You. You knew what I needed; to get still and feel Your presence. It is enough. I also want to relinquish my mission back to You. I cannot accomplish it. I give up. I cannot bring it about. I know that now.

As I left my prayer closet, I was impressed with two scriptures and hoped they might answer some of my questions and sharing.

Psalm 131:

My heart is not proud, O Lord,

my eyes are not haughty;

I do not concern myself with great matters or things too wonderful for me.

But I have stilled and quieted my soul like a weaned child with its mother,

like a weaned child is my soul within me.

O Israel, put your hope in the Lord both now and forevermore.

God had me just where I needed to be. I was confined at home so I would be forced to stop running. It was time to receive healing, and obtain what I had been asking for all along. I believe this scripture was telling me not to be proud or concern myself with great exploits but to settle in and trust Him to fulfill His promise to me. We are to wean ourselves from our fleshly desires.

The next scripture seems to follow the first. When you do these things, then this will happen:

God will change your situation and give you a new name. We go from sinner to saint, from wrecked to redeemed, from barren to fruitful. In Isaiah 62:4 we see that the land was once called *Desolate*, and is now called *Beulah*. Your land is married, it says. You are no longer walking your path alone; your relationship is restored to the Lord. He is happy with you by His side. You are married to your Maker.

And just like in a marriage, we must put our mate, our Maker, first. I repented of those things that were first in my life, pledging to make God my all in all. He would take first position, and people, projects and possessions would come behind in proper order. Suddenly, the Hosea 2:16 passage made sense to me:

In that day, declares the Lord, *you will call me 'my husband'; you will no longer call me 'my master.'*

What a tender love song. It's a love song from God to his unfaithful wife, Israel, a song of undying love. God never gives up on us, no matter how wretched and self-centered we are.

You might be in a valley of Achor right now. Perhaps you are in the midst of a personal trial or facing unbearable burdens. Then this promise in Hosea is for you. In the midst of trouble, the Lord is saying: You are my bride. I still love you. Press into Me. No matter how much you feel you've failed.

He is promising fruitfulness and hope.

I began by telling you about my Master's *decree*, and now everything I have been through points to making a deeper commitment to God.

There's security in knowing this. Every one of us knows that true happiness doesn't only come from a relationship with a man but from an intimate relationship with God. We all long for a deep, soul bond with another, but once we are fulfilled with God first, we find an abiding happiness and peace that cannot be shaken and healthier relationships with others as a result.

CHAPTER THIRTEEN

A Kink in my Plan

Dear friends, do not be surprised at the painful trial you are suffering, as if something strange were happening to you. But rejoice that you participate in the sufferings of Christ, so that you may be overjoyed when His glory is revealed. I Peter 4:12-13

When our landlord transferred to Chicago with American Airlines, he informed us we had to move; he was putting our leased house up for sale. After weeks of looking for suitable housing, no new rental turned up in the school district we desired. The boys would start high school soon and I could finally give up homeschooling. And I had so many plans for my free time. Meanwhile, we moved in with Alan's mother for the summer. His father had recently died, and there was plenty of available space.

This was temporary. We can all endure the temporary. And God was surely providing.

And then the unexpected; my mother-in-law needed my undivided and selfless attention. After a succession of orthopedic surgeries—culminating in a broken neck and near paralysis—she needed a caregiver, whose name became Holly. Yes, *me*, her *primary* caregiver. I had no experience nursing the aged, but I learned very quickly about on the job training.

There went my dreams, on the altar of surrender.

I smiled on the outside and did a bit of *whining* on the inside. Uncomfortable was an understatement. Of course, I didn't know it at the time, but my discomfort morphed into my training ground for transformation. You may know the verse in Philippians 3:10, *I want to know Him and the power of His resurrection.* But we tend to forget what follows, *And the fellowship of His suffering*.

Fellowship, companionship. If we are to fully understand what Christ endured on the cross, we need to know what it is like to go through tribulations and learn to endure as He did.

I wasn't quite there yet. Honestly, I began to lose hope—yet again—in this new kink in my plan, the suspension of my dreams. I'm sure this has happened to you, too. You've probably heard this old saying: Make plans, but write them in *pencil.* Life is so uncertain.

Proverbs 6:9, *We make plans, but the Lord directs our steps.*

Now that I was chief caregiver and knew my stay at Ida's would be more than *temporary*, I really poured on the prayer. I felt pain and loss as each month ticked by because we were in our early forties and had plenty of life ahead. I had no idea how long we would be here or when we could afford to move either. It was nothing against my mother-in-law; I was grateful to have a place but the lack of privacy to be able to talk openly at meals with my own family was lost as well as entertaining friends.

My sons needed a car for high school. Alan and I were still sharing a vehicle. We left a $315,000 designer decorated home (1988), went on a ministry venture to KC, and landed in the back two bedrooms of my mother-in-law's house. It was a bit of a shock.

I jogged to Chisholm Park to *discuss* things with God. I read Matthew 6:33 that morning and meditated on it slowly: *Seek first the kingdom of God and all these things will be added unto you also.*

I honestly prayed and repeated to the Lord His word which made this promise. I mentioned our need for vehicles and desiring a home of our own again. I wanted to participate in His kingdom on earth. I did not want to worry and try to obtain all these things for myself but trust Him to meet these needs as I put Him first.

Lord, I need your help to keep me from desiring all these material things I see others enjoying around me. Take those desires away; help me to be content, provide as You see fit.

As I continued jogging, I felt a peace about my prayer. Suddenly, right before me in a clearing of the park at 7:00 a.m., two large gates were opening at the center towards me. I saw Bonnie, my mentor, who was now deceased, inside the gates, motioning for me to enter.

“Come, come,” she said. Bonnie was clapping her hands overhead and looking towards the heavens as she used to do during worship at our church. As I passed through the gates, she began applauding again, saying,

“Welcome to the *City of Truth.*”

That was it. The vision vanished. I never had a vision nor have I since but was encouraged as I pondered this scene. Bonnie was already inside the gates, which she was, in heaven, and motioned me to come in and be welcomed. She seemed jubilant that I had made this leap of faith to the *City of Truth*. Perhaps my prayer granted me entrance to a faith filled provision or a different way of thinking. What was the *City of Truth*? I didn't know...

Later that day, I was reading *Zechariah* in the Bible. When I came to Chapter 8, the passage quoted God's declaration,

I will return to Zion and dwell in Jerusalem, the City of Truth and the mountain of the Lord will be called the Holy Mountain.
Zech. 8:3 (NASB)

God would dwell in the faithful city. When I looked up Holy Mountain, it said: *dedicated, sanctuary, consecrated.* I was stunned by the way God made His word come alive. I had no idea there was a *City of Truth* in Scripture. This treasure hunt for the riches of Christ proved the most exciting in my life thus far. Zion means *dry place*. The passage spoke of God's return to restore and refresh the apple of His eye again. The passage goes on to instruct people to speak truth to each other, judge with truth for peace in your gates. Zech. 8:16 (NASB)

Would He return to us as we became more stable, firm in our faith, truthful, and set apart for Him? Paul says in Galatians 1:10, *Am I now trying to win the approval of men, or of God*?

A few months later, one of Alan's business associates, Scott, gave us his car, an *Infinity*. Next, my sister sent me a whole suitcase of beautiful clothes, and my son won a Go Cart from *Grubbs Nissan* in a drawing he was able to turn into cash.

God was proving He wanted to take care of us and would not leave us. It didn't mean we wouldn't face difficulty but He would go through it with us.

I had a desire to speak and lead women. A God-given desire. But here I was, nursing my mother-in-law through her many orthopedic surgeries. Being stuck in the house didn't help my outlook. With my husband's dwindling real estate career, things looked a bit bleak for our family.

I'm afraid I flunked the good attitude test.

On the bright side, I wrote in my journals endlessly. I have never prayed more for our whole generational family. My church work, especially counseling prayer, continued at Restoration church. An unseen benefit began to emerge. God changed my mother-in-law's perspective, and my endurance in the situation had a good influence on my whole family.

God began teaching me to love a variety of people.

Whenever you face a situation that forces you to change your plans and die to your dreams, it's vital to cling to the truth: You are in training for something greater. It's comforting to study the story of Joseph. His tragedies and triumphs helped me to continue serving at church despite my confinement.

But my confinement, as it were, viewed as a training ground changed my outlook. It helped me believe, that someday, when God opened doors, I might be an instrument to help others, especially my family to become whole and healed.

Travis, Ida, and Spencer at her home

CHAPTER FOURTEEN

Mission Revealed

For the Lord has chosen Zion, He has desired it for his dwelling. Psalm 132:13

Sometimes when you need a piece of the big puzzle, you receive a vision or a dream. For me it was a glimpse back to my past struggle of finding and accepting my own identity. I'd like to share this dream—which is still so vivid after so long—with you.

I am in the passenger side of Joni's car. No one is driving. The car is traveling down a bumpy trail, almost automatically. I am not in control and the trail is bumpy because—it is *not my trail.*

I had been trying to do things Joni's way.

When I reach over and put my hands on the steering wheel, the car instantly turns 180 degrees in the opposite direction. What did this show me? When I accept who *I* am and the gifts God has for *me*, the car will turn toward *my* destiny.

My sister and I are different people. Her pattern, her choices, her path will not work for *me*.

It seems so simple, but it's been a hard lesson for me to learn.

During the dream, I enter a three-tiered slide which resembles a Wet'n'Wild slide. Yes, just like my journey, I remember thinking. A wet and wild roller coaster.

I see many cars going up this slide at various speeds. All seem to be proceeding at their own pace. Some cars lose ground and slide backwards a bit and start again at a snail's pace.

I floor the accelerator, doing all I can to expedite the process. I find myself at the top. It is almost as if I finish this leg of the journey. I pull into a covered driveway and an attendant comes out to park my car in a large garage area. I wonder, is this the kingdom of God? Many others have made the climb and the valet is waiting to park their cars.

Entering the building I see different rooms for different services. Two distinct destinations catch my eye. Room 101 is labeled *Healing*. There is a long line of people waiting for that room. Someone points down the hall to room 202 for *Assignments*. I go through that door and sit down in a comfortable lounge chair alone.

Two olive skinned girls enter the room wearing beautifully embroidered peasant shirts. I think of the verse in James 2:5:

Has God not chosen those who are poor in the eyes of the world to be rich in faith and to inherit the kingdom He promised those who love Him?

Are these angels or servants? They are humble and loving. They begin massaging my feet, as if to prepare me for a pedicure. It feels so good since I could not afford any pampering these last few years. I feel exhausted from my journey and sink into my chair, completely relaxed as a conversation begins.

"Who are you? How did you get here?" one girl asks.

"I was going to ask you that," I reply.

"I came as fast as I could. I pressed the gas pedal completely to the floor."

"That took a lot of courage! I came gradually; it seemed so steep and scary. There were a lot of ups and downs."

The other servant breaks in excitedly,

"I know who you are!" She stares at a list on a clipboard.

"Who?" I am overwhelmed that these servants representing the God of the universe might know me.

"You are part of the *groom's tent making committee*. Yes, you are a little apprentice, welcome."

Though I didn't know fully what that meant; it struck such a chord that I wept in overflowing joy and answered,

"Yes, that's right, I *am!* I want to learn all I can." They proceed to explain that Jesus is the groom and He is looking for a group to prepare the church to become His Bride and a place He can dwell. My exact prayers were to become a resting place or habitation for the Lord and to prepare others to be committed to Him as a bride.

The next segment of the dream (I tend to dream in scenes) included a huge white wedding cake with a Ziploc see-through cover preserving it. Seems I got to take a taste. It was the wedding cake for all the brides of the church who were being prepared to be married to their Maker. They were *being built together to become a place God lives by His Spirit*. (Eph. 2:22) Jesus was looking for a bride who would put Him first.

I felt glad to be a part of preparing others in this process. Many would come to the end of their own strength so they could be empowered by His.

Plain pots—simple and ordinary—but with a purpose grand and beautiful. So many of us feel God can't use us, or won't use us, because we're not perfect. I hope by now you know that is a lie. I love the image of being a cracked pot, containers that God wants to fill with his light and presence. A simple pot prepared to house a treasure, the Holy Spirit. As you allow God to carry His goodness and leak out into a dark world, so many other cracked pots will see God's promises for them despite their weakness.

It's been a life-changing experience for me, coming to understand that my trials, my disappointments and my detours in life can be redeemed for others.

Dear God,

Forgive me for competing with my sister. This only leads to frustration and failure. I could never live up to her and now I know I am not supposed to! Now I can rest in my own calling-confident that no one can do what You made me to do. Joni and I can rejoice in each other's different tasks. Comparison and jealousy is a scheme by the enemy that only sidetracked and delayed my own destiny.

Your word tells us to love our neighbor as ourselves. We are to follow You and not be concerned with what You are doing with another.

I feel like I've learned these lessons now and I want to help prepare the way for You to come more powerfully and deeply in women's lives, that they could have a sense of their own being and clarity in their identity and call. I want to help unite and love them and break down the barriers that I experienced earlier in my life. I want to be, as T.D. Jakes said, "like Naomi, who became so overjoyed with helping Ruth find her destiny that it broke off her chains of sorrow from her past. She began flowing again with good counsel and anointing."

Help me to condense the time it takes others to make these discoveries. Thank you for answering my prayers and showing me what work you've prepared for me to do.

In Jesus name,

Amen

The next morning I called my sister. I couldn't contain my excitement. I wanted to tell her that I had finally found my mission—perfectly tailored for me. But more than that, I needed to apologize for trying to emulate her life.

"I was never able to do it, Joni."

And guess what? Joni had something to admit to me, too. She had felt envious of my gifts and talents as well. Who would have guessed that my beautiful and accomplished sister could be threatened by me in some areas too?

The contention between us was instantly broken. By *one* phone call, one *moment* of vulnerability, of being authentic with each other at last. In that moment, my sister transformed from my biggest rival into my greatest cheerleader. She began sending designer clothes, flight tickets to visit, illustrative cards with encouragement to follow my dream and mission till completion, and finally, a sister book that is priceless. One page says, "Even though sisters appear to be sewn from a different pattern, they have a common thread that can't be broken by people or years or distance."

All those years I assumed things about her that simply weren't there. And all the while she longed for a sister-bond with me.

Joni and Holly, Sister Book

A Common Thread, Girls With Grandmother

CHAPTER FIFTEEN

Sister Love Revived

Let us therefore make every effort to do what leads to peace and to mutual edification. Romans 14:19

It was summer 2007 when Joni and I had this amazing conversation. I still lived at my mother-in-law's as her caregiver. Joni proposed a plan; she and I would go to Houston for an early Christmas with our Mom and her husband, Ken, with plenty of time for me to return and join my own family. Since we lived in different areas of the country, we seldom had a chance to be together. Joni wanted this to be a special Christmas, with fun activities and programs like we once had in our neighborhood.

"Let's pantomime a song of our choice, act it out, and sing some carols," she suggested. Works for me and always has. Our sister act revised.

Alan and I were still in the middle of some financial struggles due to the dismal state of the real estate market. Money was tight. Keeping my chin up proved a real choice. We had no idea what our next step would be. Making a trip to Houston was a stretch, but I needed to go.

On Christmas Eve I walked into Mom's house, took one look at the Christmas tree and exclaimed, "Wow! Look at all the presents."

When we passed out packages, my pile grew higher and higher. Overwhelmed with emotion and teary, I said, "It's just too much. I can't accept these."

Joni showered me with most of the gifts, not practical things or simple-hearted gifts, as was our family tradition. No, these were gifts meant to spoil me. From her closet she'd gathered jackets, jewelry, leather handbags, blouses, sweaters and shipped them ahead to Mom's house. We're talking designer boutique-style items, not ordinary hand-me-downs. These were expensive.

I came with only the usual heart gifts for the others. I was embarrassed and humbled to receive so much. Mom saw the signs and whispered,

"Don't spoil your sister's joy of giving."

Suddenly my face brightened, I tore through the paper and cried as I *oohed* and *aahed* over each piece. I couldn't wait to try on the clothes and jewelry. After slipping back into the bedroom,

I emerged to model each of the ensembles. My whole countenance changed into joyful excitement. "Remember our Sears Charm School days, Sis?" I said. "Am I walking like a lady?" I modeled each outfit with those pronounced stances, the way we'd learned to carry ourselves with style, charm, and poise. Whirling and showing off, removing jackets and hamming it up brought us all to giggling so hard we couldn't catch our breath. We sang carols, acted out our special song, and danced around the room to the stereo music.

The magic of Christmas is really about giving. That's what Mom had taught us for all those years.

I was the lucky recipient of Joni's expression of love and generosity. Not everyone can have such a sister as Joni, nor have a restoration story as we now have. You may be still waiting to resolve a difference with a sibling or loved one. But God's desire is to restore, to mend what is broken, and He is constantly working to bring this about. Even when we can't see it. Perhaps you are estranged from someone in your family and missing the love and closeness. Have hope, believe in God's promises, and keep on the lookout for those surprise friends that He will bring into your life to shower His gifts upon you.

Holly modeling her gifts

CHAPTER SIXTEEN

Time to Tell Your Story

Write down the revelation and make it plain on tablets so that a herald may run with it.
Habakkuk 2:2

Shortly after the holiday, I attended a women's conference called *Pink Impact* at *Gateway Church* in Southlake. Its theme: to encourage women that they can make a difference.

Standing in a sea of worshiping women, I still felt *alone*. I silently dialogue with God about my journey and the fact that the ministry I envisioned had not materialized after many years. I stated that I would now pass my journals of life lessons to my sons and forget about helping women in a greater capacity. I heard a whisper, *Something more... it's time to tell your story*.

My *conversation* was interrupted by the speaker encouraging us to share and write our story. I'd been journaling for years, simply to record my experiences and process everything inside me, but I suddenly put it all together. The journaling had a *purpose*. A new zeal *awakened* in me, new desires ignited.

Not only did the speaker encourage women to tell their story, but as an outline for the process, she used as examples every Scripture I had clung to over the past five years. *Wow*. God had my attention. Any one of us can teach and share our story. God's story—of redemption, healing, and transformation—is written through the fabric of our *lives*.

Many of us, the speaker added, have a bruised image of ourselves. We're intimidated by speaking. Oh, how true is that? Bruised image—cracked pots. Yes, many women are living in isolation, on a hidden journey with the Lord, and so hesitant to share with others. Many simply need to feel accepted, valued and confident.

I want to help them prime the pump. I was awakening to purpose again.

Lisa Bevere, our speaker, was very forthright,

"Women are sometimes slanderous, mean, jealous, backbiting, and competitive." Have you come across women whom you trust that betray you, talk behind your back, pretend to care but ignore you? Women are often in competition with other women. They distrust other women because—after all—they've been betrayed by those they trusted. Once I recalled how God helped me conquer those attitudes toward other women in my own life—and family—I knew my calling.

During our break, Lisa suggested an exercise: we were to find a woman and tell her something we really admire about her, affirm her.

This is the exact opposite of comparing yourself to a woman, feeling envious of what she has that you don't. Compliment, don't compete.

If we are the only ones that can do the mission we are created to do, there is no reason to compete. Have you ever thought of it that way? Why not encourage and build up the Body of Christ? If we make a united effort to make a difference in the lives of others, isn't it a stand against the enemy? I am convinced we can defeat the enemy this way. When we break down barriers of feeling slighted and overcome with admiration and love, we see a tapestry of the manifold wisdom of God.

We each have a part. *Your story matters.*

When we see someone overcome adversity in their life, doesn't it inspire us to persevere? I knew then and there that God had something for me greater than I could imagine.

I needed to trust and wait.

When the break in the conference came, I glanced across the room to see whom I would go to encourage. I spotted Mary Forsythe, author of *A Glimpse of Grace*. I had just read her book which encouraged me in ways no one could fathom. As I made my way over to tell her what an impact her book had made on my life, it came to me that when we can relate to another's experience, it gives us courage to move forward and believe for the impossible in our own lives.

Mary had a riches to rags (Beverly Hills lifestyle) story where she lost everything. To top it off, she ended up in prison on an unintentional fraud charge through the pharmacy she owned. In her cell, she had an encounter with God. A man was sent to pray for her, and through him God filled Mary with His spirit. She received a mandate for women nationwide.

After her release, she began a speaking ministry. Women are set free from their emotional and spiritual bondage through her message. That's how He redeems what we have lost, restores what has been devoured.

Mary's testimony gave me hope that all of life is a *school* and God has a purpose for our confinement, our waiting time. A friend of mine likens it to a holding pattern, like an airplane circling the runway waiting for clearance to land. All those months behind bars became Mary's preparation for the encounter, the catapult, into destiny. Read her story. It will encourage you to stay on course as it did for me when I felt confined, caring for my mother-in-law after she broke her neck.

Looking back I see it as simply a part of the training. As if I were sitting on the bench waiting to get into the game. Waiting on God's timing for His empowerment of the message I desired for women to hear. He was definitely doing some refining work in all of our lives.

CHAPTER SEVENTEEN

Hidden Voices Inspiration

But when you pray, go into your room, close the door and pray to your Father, who is unseen. Then your Father, who sees what is done in secret, will reward you. Matthew 6:6

I left the conference reignited and excited that at last God was going to help me tell my story. However, I realized my speaking skills were a bit rusty, and the idea of standing on a stage or behind a podium was highly intimidating. So if I had these issues, a girl who put on plays in her garage, wouldn't other women too?

And if they remained frightened to share, the enemy would win. No, we have to overcome the enemy through our testimonies. That alone is enough reason for more women to learn to be open and vulnerable.

It's been said that you teach what you most need to learn, so I started a speaking group in my church, to help women experience the redemptive potential in the hardships they endured. Colleen Foshee, a speaker for ProvenWay ministries, led the group with me. With her encouragement, organization, (I so needed that) and experience, we made it work.

We desired to help the women find their voice and gain confidence to speak. I started the group in a real step of faith because I was anxious about public speaking myself. I believed God prompted me that it was time to tell my story, and that He would give the ability to do it.

And it's much more fun to practice together as a group.

I found all the scriptures in the Bible which illustrated how God gave Moses, Paul, and other Bible characters the ability to do what He was calling them to do regardless of their ability. Encouragement starts with Scripture.

Even though our stories were only 5-10 minutes long each month, I often could not sleep the night before my turn because of a fear of failure. Shyness took over. When I did speak, my hands were clammy and my heart was racing. Colleen told me, "The nervousness will wear off. Speaking is a process."

It was a magical time to hear the women's inspiring stories and the sometimes painful communication turning into exhilaration as each story surfaced and encouraged another through a current trial. I didn't want another woman to sit out in the audience of a conference and think their time had passed and there was no place available to activate their dream. I was going to use the authority I had to help women condense the time to reach their purpose, acquire the skills to tell their story, and bring the isolated back in circulation by hearing stories of faith. I desired for every woman to find their identity, gain confidence, and reach their full potential.

Persistence and *practice* are the key. Could it be that Mrs. Arthur, my fourth grade teacher was right? You must practice and develop your gift. This proved to be the advice I needed for myself and the rest of the group. Learn and grow through your mistakes and flaws.

My message was evolving from my weakness and a place of defeat. I needed to take responsibility not to be lazy and microwave minded. It actually helped the group to know I was a vulnerable novice like many of them. We would learn together. There were all different types of women who came, every nationality and age; some beginners, some seasoned that were staying sharp for their next engagement.

God gave me a simple format to help draw out these stories. *Begin sharing in a relaxed way, over coffee, as if catching up with a best girlfriend.*

If being involved in a group like this inspires you, consider enlisting women to begin meeting together. Set up standards and practices from the beginning. First, absolutely no competition between you. Believe me, it happens to the best of us. We look at an accomplished speaker and tell ourselves we can never be polished and speak as eloquently as she does.

No, decide that each of you has a unique contribution to make. Vow to create a spirit of love and encouragement. The more experienced will help the beginners. One night all our stories fit together into a complete message. We left the meeting elated, revived as each shared their journey and God's faithfulness to them.

I'm sure you have an incredible testimony, too, but it may be hidden beneath fear and maybe even shame. God wants to use your trials and your flaws. It isn't about your story, but about what God has done *through it*.

A year later I started a ministry called *Hidden Voices* with ProvenWay Ministries as my sponsor. I want to help women find their voice *till we all have voices*. Women want to unite and share transparently, and need a safe atmosphere to do it.

If you're interested, I have a free download of the format and values we stressed in our first group on my website for you to start your own group in your church.

I encourage you to take the *Strengthfinders 2.0* test by Tom Rath. You'll see if your talents line up with your work and what you were best created to do.

Women from our group began to plug into their place of service and flourish. Many branched out in acting, missions, prison ministry, speaking, authors, teaching, social media, Bible study leaders, organizations like Jews for Jesus, India missions. Some became church planters, and even guests and hosts for Christian radio and TV stations. Amazing. Faith building.

And it had nothing to do with me. I just followed God's lead, my passion, and God did the rest. These women were headed toward their purpose regardless. Together we began to *fan our gift into flame* by practice. (II Tim. 1:6) I then passed them on to the excellent women in leadership development at Gateway Church. (W.I.L.D.)

Wendy hosts Gateway Practice Group

Dorothy hosts Gateway group 2010

CHAPTER EIGHTEEN

Rebuilt, Refined, Re-fired in His Image

Arise, shine for your light has come, and the glory of the Lord rises upon you. Isaiah 60:1

Last summer while visiting family in Santa Fe with Joni, we found ourselves in an art museum. Across the room I spotted a pot under Plexiglas. Its unusual beauty drew me to admire it. We later learned the story behind the creation. While the potter crafted the pot, it exploded in his hands. Instead of discarding the disaster, he decided to gather the hundred pieces on the ground and glue them back together. Then he re-fired, repainted, restored and reassembled the pot.

I've never seen something so stunning. (see front cover) It proved a wonderful method for the potter to display his skill and handiwork. It was far more beautiful than before.

And from then on the potter changed his style. Now, he puts all his creations through this very same process. They have a design quality and uniqueness that reflects their maker like never before. He breaks them on purpose before rebuilding and *re-firing* them.

Doesn't God do the same for us? I heard Pastor Chuck Swindoll say once that God uses adversity to break our self-will and transform us into useful vessels. It's the way He deals with our self-reliance. Brokenness is not about punishment. It's an act of love and mercy. Moses was broken in the desert and spent forty years learning to obey the Lord. The apostle Paul had a "thorn in the flesh" that kept this once-arrogant man eternally humble. And look at Peter. Jesus corrected his pride many times, so he could eventually lead the entire church.

Brokenness is a *gift*. It helps us see our shortcomings, our own sin. It allows us to have compassion for others. It helps us serve Him more effectively and display His kingdom despite our weaknesses. We become re-fired, refined, and renewed. He changes our image, our names and our motives to reflect a glory that shines for others.

And we, who with unveiled faces all reflect the Lord's glory, are being transformed into His likeness with ever-increasing glory, which comes from the Lord, who is the Spirit. 2 Cor. 3:18

LESSONS FROM A CRACKED POT

We do not need degrees to follow God's plan. But we do need a willing heart. He longs to teach us how to untangle the mess in our lives. As you know, I struggled with faulty thinking. I couldn't find the answers in any how-to book, only through the Bible and what it revealed to me.

"*God wants us to know the love that surpasses knowledge.*" (Eph. 3:19) He will put people in your path that may be a bit "prickly." Author Joyce Landorf calls them "irregular people." How else can we learn to love those who are different? We are to look beyond the thorns into the treasure of each heart.

Perhaps there are people you need to "love" back into life, to help them on the journey of healing and hope. God will give you new eyes to see the goodness in someone that you may just as well want to cast off. Remember the potter? He saw treasure in the broken pieces and began the painstaking work of making them into something of value.

God taught me not to be who I think I should be. No one can bond with a false mask or a shell of a person who has lost her voice and sense of being. Your highest calling is to be who God made you to be.

Don't we all have a need for significance? We're wired to be valued and acknowledged. In God's kingdom, significance comes about when there is more of Him and less of me.

We can't be good in our own strength. We're programmed to be self-serving. But God is good, and He has a plan. I am no longer following a rulebook because He is writing the guidebook for my journey. He's writing it on my heart and by His Spirit.

He'll write *yours* too.

Transcending the world's values and ambitions to come into our true inheritance of trust and dependence is a daily challenge and a narrow path that few find.

Humbling ourselves and making the first move to resolve offenses can turn your biggest rival into your greatest cheerleader. Leave the rest to God. When you do, doors of opportunity open and your voice returns.

God is gracious to show us that He will take all of the pieces of our broken lives and rebuild and restore them to display His beauty even more effectively to reach others. We are all flawed and it is good to come to terms with our humanity.

You may have wondered why you ended up in your family, but after struggling with those "why" questions, I've come to see that God never makes a mistake. We are born into our family for a divine purpose. How wonderful it is to begin to thank Him instead of complaining.

Cease striving to accomplish only what God can do. God often causes men and women to exhaust their reservoir of effort before He replaces it with His own ability.

My prayers were answered by roads paved with hardships but they required me to make changes I would never make on my own otherwise.

Develop a tough skin but keep a tender heart. We aren't to compete or judge but to communicate, be truthful, and real. We must see from God's perspective because when we judge, we perpetuate the cycle of behavior we'd like to end.

We must become still enough to receive His plan. He can't give a moving target His agenda. The turtle beat the hare after all, didn't he?

There is a difference in knowledge and wisdom. Knowledge comes from facts; wisdom from life experience.

Pride is the biggest enemy to growth.

Embrace your thorns. Why? Because painful circumstances, mean people who have offended you or spoken falsely about you are actually helping you arrive sooner to your destination. They are helping us to die to our self and reputation in the world and, as a result, bring the humility necessary to hold the gift God has for us. If we are made in the image of Christ and follow in His footsteps, we must remember that He was made of no reputation. God is renaming all of us as we come through our trials. He is making us into the women He created us to be.

Humility is the key to this journey. We are all flawed. Sometimes we have to live with a limp in the area of our natural strength, like Jacob. Only then are we forced to depend on God.

Learn to see from the eyes of your heart the beauty in people and His kingdom. God teaches us to rest in Him in quiet and trust. He sends us to help others find their shoes to fit their spiritual walk and place of service.

Our inadequacies actually qualify us for ministry. The more broken we are of our strength, the more He can flow through us.

I spent so many years questioning God, and my journey which I have just shared with you took me on many roads through many years to find the answers. It was not the journey I envisioned, but in the end I welcome every step, even every misstep.

Listen for His voice and begin your journey. The things you learn along the way are not only for you—your healing and restoration—but for those you'll meet along the way. The world needs your inspiration and impact and the life-giving message that God is writing through you. I can't wait to read your life-giving message.

Because the Sovereign Lord helps me, I will not be disgraced. Therefore have I set my face like flint, and I know I will not be put to shame. He who vindicates me is near. Is. 50:7

Holly W. Smith

ACTIVATION PRAYER

1. Lord, thank you for who you made me to be in Christ. I know that you are the Potter, and I am the clay. You have a unique plan for my life. Help me to know that I am the only one who can fulfill my mission and there is no need to compare myself with others or compete for love or attention. Forgive me from envy because your Word says that if there is still jealousy among us we are worldly. Help me to see Your kingdom and rejoice in others' success because we each have a part to play. Let me be known for my love and acceptance of others just as the disciples were recognized by their love for one another. Help others to see Christ in me, my hope of glory.

2. Lord, I ask You to fill me with Your spirit and move me to follow your decrees. As I obey your guidance, help me become all You created me to be. As I discover my gifts, help me take responsibility to practice and develop them, to fan

them into flame according to II Tim. 1:6. We don't want to be lazy but to imitate those who through faith and patience inherit what has been promised. (Heb. 6:12)

3. Help me to forgive those who have offended me even if it wasn't my fault so that I am free for Your blessing. Making the first move requires humility so I pray for that grace. Your word reminds me in I Peter 5:6, as I humble myself, in due time You will raise me up. Thank You for revealing rivals that unearthed envy in me so I can confess my sin and have a heart change to love. You have a plan for my freedom.

4. Help me to line up those areas of self-will with Your will and surrender control for You to have Your way in my life. Turn the shame of inadequacy and imperfections into a channel to deliver Your message more fully and effectively as I depend on You.

5. Help me to cease striving to fulfill my own destiny and focus on my relationship with You. Help me to come to terms with my flaws and know there is only One who is perfect. Thank You that Your power is made perfect in my weakness. Forgive me for wrong motives of selfish ambition or wanting to make a name for myself. Help me to only be concerned with making Your name significant.

6. We know according to Hebrews 4:12 that you judge the thoughts and attitudes of the heart.

Grant me pure motives and overcoming attitudes that I remember who I am assigned to not what You can do for me. Help me to complete my goals, projects and finish my work.

7. Help me to remember to praise You because I am fearfully and wonderfully made. (Ps. 139:14) You are worthy, O Lord to receive all the glory and honor and power, for You created all things and by Your will they were created and have their being. (Rev. 3:11)

8. Fill me with Your Holy Spirit.

REFERENCES

Chapter 1: "Everybody is a Star", Sly & the Family Stone, lyrics found at metrolyrics.com

Chapter 2: *The Matrix* by the Wachowski Brothers Oct. 2008

Chapter 8: Ortberg, John; *Everybody's Normal Till You Get to Know Them*; Zondervan, Michigan 2003

Chapter 9: Cracked Pots Painting by David Caris, 1986

Chapter 16: A Glimpse of Grace by Mary Forsythe, www.kingdomliving.org

Chapter 17: *Strengthfinders 2.0* by Tom Rath tomrath.org

Lessons from a Cracked Pot: "Irregular People" by Joyce Landorf

Chapter 16: Lisa Bevere quote and directives, "Pink Impact" at Gateway Church 2007

ABOUT THE AUTHOR

Holly writes for *Powerfuljourneymag.com* and speaks for *ProvenWay Ministries* at *Hope Center* in Plano, Texas. She founded *Hidden Voices Ministry* in 2009 to help women find their voice and gain confidence in speaking their stories. She believes every story is valuable and redemptive for others. Her teachings reflect her struggles and the transformation God brought in her life. She is currently a transformational coach and mentor for women. She serves as a volunteer at *Gateway Church*, in Southlake, Texas. She has been married to Alan for 32 years and has two grown sons. She resides in the Dallas Fort Worth area.

To contact the author: www.hollywsmith.com

Holly W. Smith

The very things which barred my way became my avenues to freedom.

-Oswald Chambers

www.ingramcontent.com/pod-product-compliance
Lightning Source LLC
Chambersburg PA
CBHW060521030426
42337CB00015B/1962

* 9 7 8 0 6 1 5 8 8 4 7 6 9 *